SPORTS
IN ACTION

LACROSSE

in Action

John Crossingham

 Crabtree Publishing Company

www.crabtreebooks.com

Created by Bobbie Kalman

Dedicated by John Crossingham
With love to the Broken Social Scene

Editor-in-Chief
Bobbie Kalman

Author
John Crossingham

Editorial director
Niki Walker

Project editor
Rebecca Sjonger

Editors
Amanda Bishop
Kathryn Smithyman

Design
Margaret Amy Reiach
Campbell Creative Services (cover)

Production coordinator
Heather Fitzpatrik

Photo research
Rebecca Sjonger

Special thanks to
Ron McSpayden

Consultant
Brian Logue, Director of Communications
US Lacrosse

Photographs and reproductions
Bruce Curtis: front cover, title page, pages 3, 4, 5 (top), 6, 8, 16, 17, 18, 21, 23, 25, 31
Ike Levine/Sports Probe (www.sportsprobe.com): pages 10, 28
©Permission of Lazare & Parker: page 5 (bottom)
PhotoDisc: back cover

Illustrations
Katherine Kantor: chapter heading, pages 13, 14, 15, 26, 27, 30, 31
Bonna Rouse: pages 7, 9, 11, 12, 16, 17, 19, 20, 22, 23, 24, 25, 29

Digtial prepress
Embassy Graphics

Printer
Worzalla Publishing Company

Crabtree Publishing Company

www.crabtreebooks.com   1-800-387-7650

Cataloging in Publication Data
Crossingham, John
   Lacrosse in action / John Crossingham

p. cm. —(Sports in action)
Includes index.

This book describes various forms of lacrosse, scoring, rules, skills, and tips for playing the
sport of lacrosse.

ISBN 0-7787-0329-0 (library bound) ISBN 0-7787-0349-5 (pbk.)
1. Lacrosse—Juvenile literature. [1. Lacrosse.] I. Title. II. Series.

GV989.17 .c76 2003
j796.34'7—dc21

**Published in
the United States**
PMB 16A
350 Fifth Ave.
Suite 3308
New York, NY
10118

**Published
in Canada**
616 Welland Ave.,
St. Catharines,
Ontario, Canada
L2M 5V6

**Published in the
United Kingdom**
73 Lime Walk
Headington
Oxford
OX3 7AD
United Kingdom

**Published
in Australia**
386 Mt. Alexander Rd.,
Ascot Vale (Melbourne)
VIC 3032

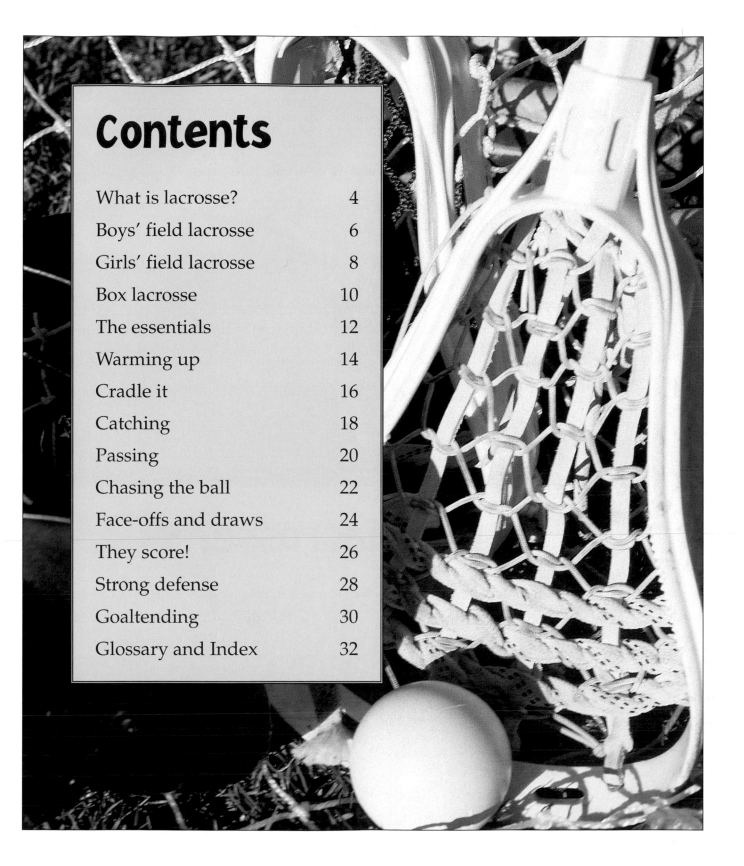

Contents

What is lacrosse?

Lacrosse is a fast-paced sport played by two teams. Each team attempts to score **goals** by getting a small ball into its opponent's **net**. The team with the most goals at the end of the game wins. Players catch, carry, pass, and shoot the ball using a long **crosse**, or stick. The stick has a handle and a netted pocket at one end for holding the ball. There are three main types of lacrosse: boys' **field lacrosse**, girls' field lacrosse, and **box lacrosse**. Field lacrosse is an outdoor sport that is played on a grass field. Box lacrosse is usually played indoors, where the game is "boxed" in by walls, but it can also be played outdoors. The walls are set up around the playing field to enclose it. Each type of lacrosse has different rules and **positions**, but they all use similar skills.

Check it out

Some lacrosse leagues allow **contact**, which means players are allowed to **body check**, or use their bodies to move opponents out of the way. Boys' field lacrosse and most box lacrosse leagues allow body checking. It is not permitted in girls' field lacrosse or in any type of league that has very young players. Neither boys nor girls are allowed to hit other players with their sticks.

(right) The girl in red has the ball, so her team is playing **offense**, *or trying to score. Her opponents are playing* **defense**. *They try to get the ball and stop the red team from scoring.*

A native history

Lacrosse is the oldest sport in North America. It was developed centuries ago by Native Americans, who called it *baggataway*. Some games had only a few players on each team. Other games had thousands of players and were played on fields that were miles long! French missionaries called *baggataway* "lacrosse" because to them the stick looked like a bishop's staff, or *crosse*. Modern lacrosse began in eastern Canada in the mid-1800s. Today lacrosse is Canada's national summer sport, and the game is quickly becoming popular in other countries.

Native Americans played baggataway *to practice for war, to settle disputes, and as part of ceremonies.*

Boys' field lacrosse

Boys' field lacrosse is the oldest version of modern lacrosse. A game lasts for four periods, called **quarters**. Men's games are an hour long, with fifteen-minute quarters. Boys' games have quarters that last from eight to twelve minutes.

Follow the rules

Men's field lacrosse has three **officials**—a **referee**, a **field judge**, and an **umpire**. Boys' field lacrosse has only one or two officials. If a player breaks a rule, he commits a **foul** and gets a **penalty** as punishment. There are two types of fouls—**personal** and **technical**.

Getting personal

Personal fouls include tripping and **slashing**, or hitting a player with your stick. If you commit a personal foul, you must leave the game for one minute. You wait in the **penalty box** while your team plays on with fewer players.

Technicalities

Technical fouls include pushing another player from behind and **holding**, or grabbing a player or his stick. If you get a technical foul, the other team gets control of the ball. You also may be sent to the penalty box, but you will only have to sit out for half a minute.

Boys' field positions

Although a team can have over twenty players, there are only ten on the playing field at once. Each one plays a certain **position**. Examine the positions on the red team. Right now, this team has the ball in its **attack half** and is playing offense. The labels on this diagram refer to the positions of players on the red team.

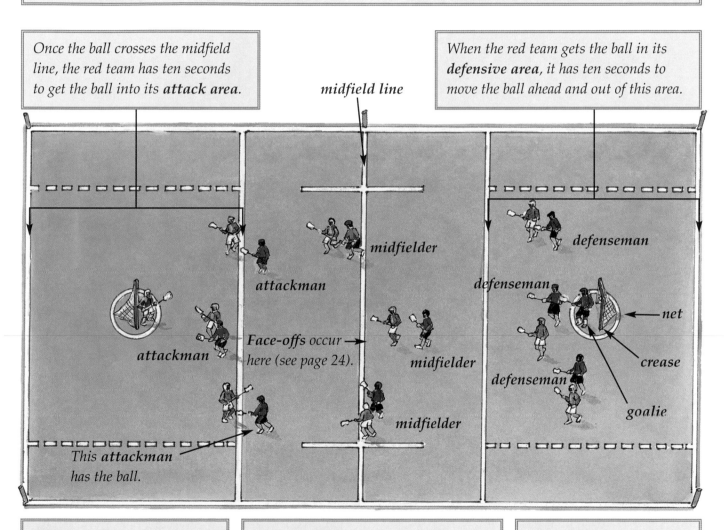

*Once the ball crosses the midfield line, the red team has ten seconds to get the ball into its **attack area**.*

midfield line

*When the red team gets the ball in its **defensive area**, it has ten seconds to move the ball ahead and out of this area.*

midfielder

attackman

defenseman

defenseman

net

attackman

Face-offs occur here (see page 24).

midfielder

crease

defenseman

goalie

midfielder

*This **attackman** has the ball.*

Three **attackmen** set up shots and try to score goals. One is the team's top scorer. These players stay on the attacking side of the midfield line.

Three **midfielders** move the ball up the field and help the defenders when the ball is in their defensive area. The two outside midfielders are also called **wings**. They can go anywhere on the field.

The **goalie** guards the net. Three **defensemen** protect and assist him. They stay on the defending side of the midfield line.

Girls' field lacrosse

Field hockey players were the first to play girls' field lacrosse. As a result, the playing field, uniforms, and some rules are similar to those of field hockey. Games in girls' field lacrosse last for two periods, called **halves**. Each half is 30 minutes long, although younger players play shorter halves. The games are usually supervised by a single umpire. Whenever the umpire blows the whistle, all players except the goalies must stop moving.

Girls' field lacrosse has two types of fouls. **Major fouls** include slashing and **charging**, or pushing an opponent. **Minor fouls** include **body balls**—using the body to knock the ball ahead—and checking an opponent's stick when it is empty. When a player gets a foul, her opponent is given a **free position**. A free position allows the opponent to shoot the ball without being checked. The punished player must stand at least thirteen feet (4 m) away.

Girls' field positions

There are twelve positions in girls' field lacrosse. Except for the goalie, each player is assigned an opponent to **mark**, or cover, on the field. Right now, the red team has the ball and is playing offense. The labels on this diagram are for players in red.

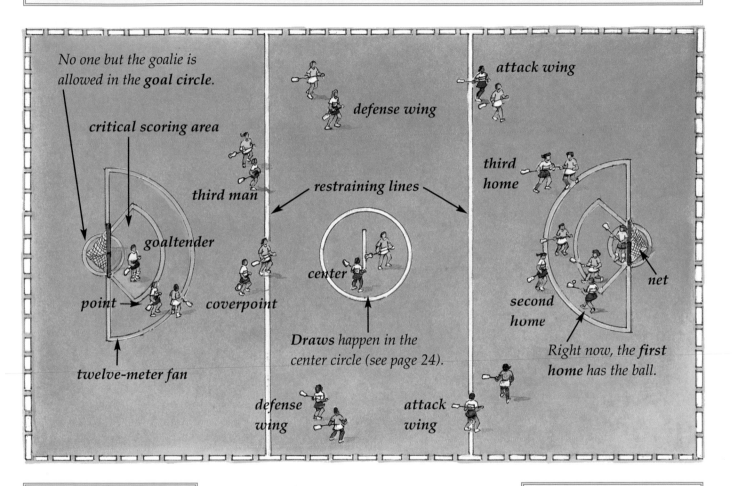

No one but the goalie is allowed in the **goal circle**.

critical scoring area

third man

goaltender

point →

coverpoint

twelve-meter fan

defense wing

restraining lines

center

Draws happen in the center circle (see page 24).

defense wing

attack wing

attack wing

third home

net

second home

*Right now, the **first home** has the ball.*

*There are six **defenders**: **point**, **coverpoint**, **third man**, two **defense wings**, and the **center**. These players try to get control of the ball and stop their opponents from scoring.*

No more than eight players from the defending team or seven players from the offensive team are allowed past a restraining line at once.

*There are five **attackers**: **first home**, **second home**, **third home**, and two **attack wings**. These players attempt to set up shots and score goals. The first home is the team's main scorer.*

9

Box lacrosse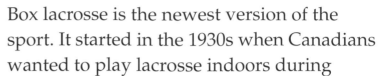

Box lacrosse is the newest version of the sport. It started in the 1930s when Canadians wanted to play lacrosse indoors during cold winters. Box lacrosse shares many characteristics with ice hockey. In fact, the game is usually played in a hockey **arena**. The playing surface is either concrete or artificial grass called **astroturf**. Unlike field lacrosse, box lacrosse is played the same way by both boys and girls.

The penalty box

Box lacrosse players commit similar fouls to field lacrosse players, but they receive slightly different penalties. A minor foul, such as slashing or tripping, puts a player in the penalty box for two minutes. A major foul, such as fighting, gets a player five minutes in the penalty box. When a player is in the penalty box, his or her team is **short-handed**, and the other team is on a **power play**.

Time is up

Another difference in box lacrosse is the use of a **shot clock**. Once a team gets the ball, it has thirty seconds to take a shot on the net. If it doesn't, the other team gets the ball. This rule makes box lacrosse a fast game!

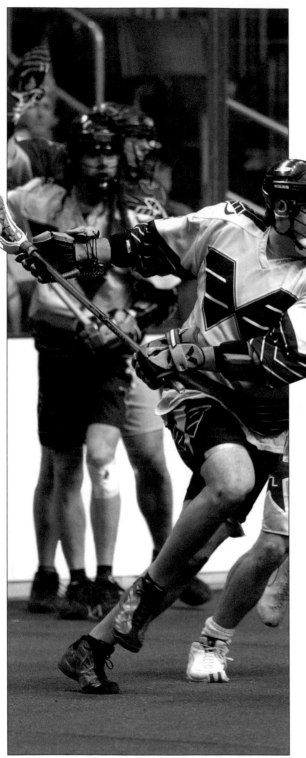

Many professional leagues in North America are box lacrosse leagues.

Box lacrosse positions

Each team has six positions on the playing field. Although professional leagues use three officials per game, most youth league games have one or two officials. In this diagram, the red team has the ball. The labels refer to positions on this team.

The **point**, or **center**, is the team's main scorer.

Two **corners** act as defenders. They also bring the ball up the floor and set up the attackers.

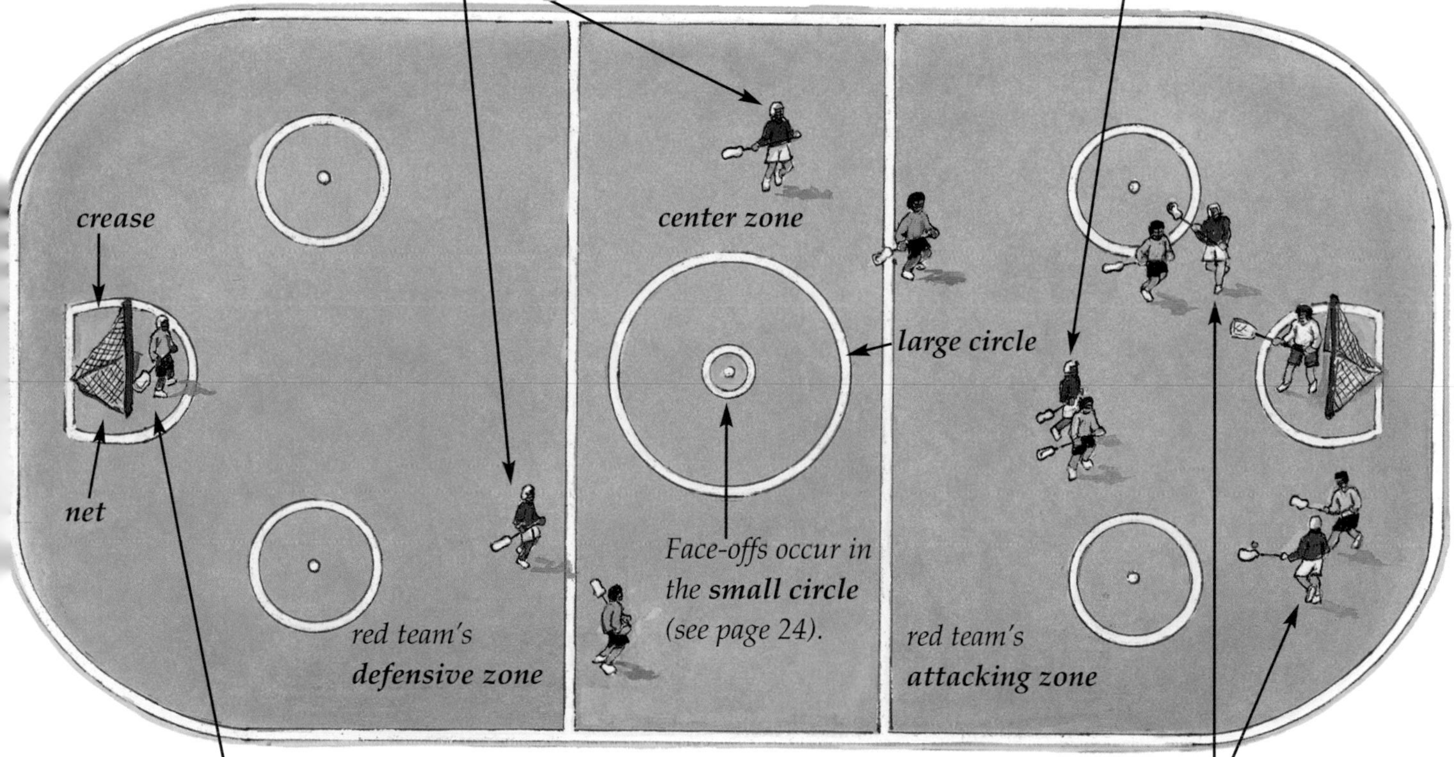

crease

center zone

large circle

net

Face-offs occur in the **small circle** (see page 24).

red team's **defensive zone**

red team's **attacking zone**

The goalie remains in the **crease** for most of the game to protect the net.

Two **crease players** cover each side of the attacking zone and attempt to score.

The essentials

Different lacrosse players use different equipment. Box lacrosse and male field lacrosse players wear equipment that is similar to that worn by ice hockey players—helmets, athletic supports, and body pads. Female field lacrosse players wear uniforms similar to those worn by field hockey players. They wear skirts with shorts underneath and usually do not wear pads. Every lacrosse player carries a stick and wears a pair of proper shoes.

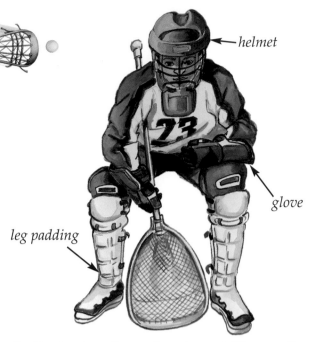

helmet

glove

leg padding

Goaltenders use the most equipment. They are the only players who wear leg padding. They also use a different style of stick than other players do.

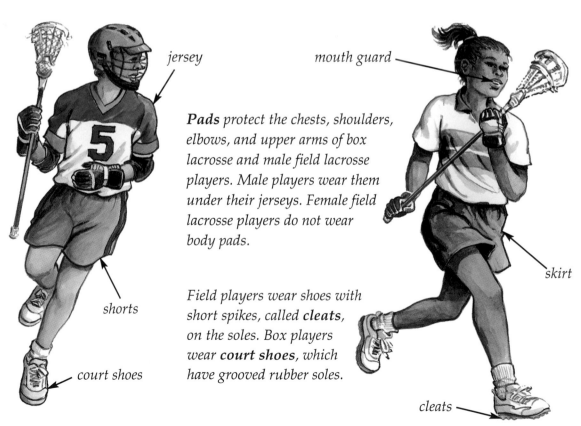

jersey

shorts

court shoes

mouth guard

skirt

cleats

Pads *protect the chests, shoulders, elbows, and upper arms of box lacrosse and male field lacrosse players. Male players wear them under their jerseys. Female field lacrosse players do not wear body pads.*

Field players wear shoes with short spikes, called **cleats***, on the soles. Box players wear* **court shoes***, which have grooved rubber soles.*

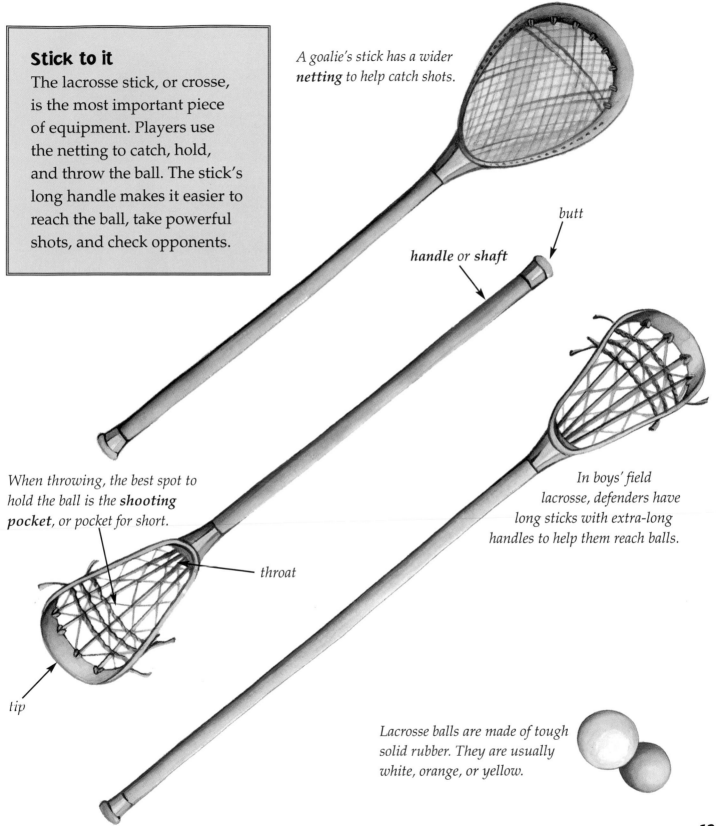

Stick to it

The lacrosse stick, or crosse, is the most important piece of equipment. Players use the netting to catch, hold, and throw the ball. The stick's long handle makes it easier to reach the ball, take powerful shots, and check opponents.

*A goalie's stick has a wider **netting** to help catch shots.*

butt

handle** or **shaft

*When throwing, the best spot to hold the ball is the **shooting pocket**, or pocket for short.*

throat

tip

In boys' field lacrosse, defenders have long sticks with extra-long handles to help them reach balls.

Lacrosse balls are made of tough solid rubber. They are usually white, orange, or yellow.

13

Warming up

It is important to stretch and warm up before practicing or playing lacrosse. Warming up loosens your muscles so you move better, and it helps prevent injuries such as muscle strains and pulls. While stretching, move slowly and don't bounce. Never stretch farther than feels comfortable.

Leg lunges

Stand with your feet wide apart. Bend your right knee until you feel a stretch on the inside of your left leg. Hold the stretch for a count of five. Straighten up and switch sides.

Neck stretch

It is easy to hurt your neck, so do this stretch carefully. Tilt your head forward so that your chin points at your chest. Slowly move your head toward one shoulder and then the other. Do not roll your head backward or farther than feels comfortable.

Arm circles

Swing your arms in large circles. Make the circles smaller and smaller until your arms are moving in tiny circles straight out at the sides. Reverse direction, starting with small movements and ending with giant circles.

Quadriceps stretch

Stand on your right foot and use your right hand to help balance yourself. Bring your left foot up behind you until you can grab it with your left hand. Pull gently until you feel the stretch in the front of your thigh. Hold the stretch for a count of ten and then stretch your right leg.

Trunk circles

Place your feet shoulder-width apart and put your hands on your hips. Keep your feet flat on the ground and swing your hips around in circles. Do three circles to the right and three to the left.

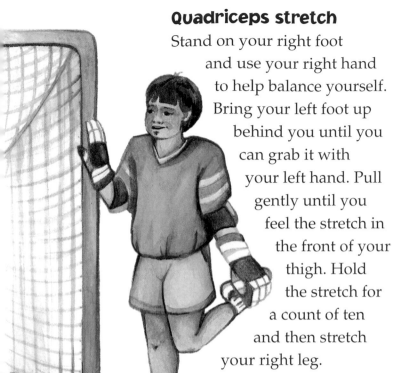

Ankle stretch

Sit on the ground with one leg straight. Bend your other leg so that you can grab your foot. Gently move it in circles. When you have done ten, stop and do ten circles in the other direction. Change legs!

"V" stretch

Sit with your legs in a "V." Stretch your arms toward your feet until you feel a stretch in the back of your legs and buttocks. Hold the stretch for a count of ten.

Cradle it

Although the rules for each style of lacrosse are different, the basic skills are the same. The first skill you should master is **cradling**. Cradling is the back-and-forth movement of your stick that allows you to keep the ball in the pocket as you run. Cradling also helps you protect the ball when your opponents check you.

Hold on

Before learning to cradle, take a moment to become familiar with holding your stick. One hand stays near the butt of the stick and helps keep it steady. This hand is your **bottom hand**. Your other hand is the **top hand**. The top hand stays near the middle of the shaft. This hand aims your shots and puts force into them. Your top hand is usually your favored hand. For example, if you are right-handed, then your right hand will probably be your top hand.

Get a feel for it

You use different cradles to position the ball in the netting. A large cradle helps hold the ball in the stick's throat as you run. A small cradle shifts the ball into the pocket, where you have the most throwing control.

Young players should remember to keep both hands on their sticks as they cradle.

To perform a small cradle, bring your stick up over the shoulder of your top hand. Move the wrist of your top hand back and forth. You will feel the ball naturally move into the pocket.

On the move

Hopping or turning while you're running can accidentally bounce the ball out of your netting. A large cradle motion keeps the ball in your stick's throat. To do a large cradle, use your fingers as well as your wrist to create an angled up-and-down motion with the stick. Your movements must be quick and smooth in order to keep the ball safely in the netting.

Hold the stick in a nearly upright position with your top hand just below the throat. Let the pocket swing out and downward by straightening the fingers of your top hand and bending your wrist. To swing the pocket up and in, quickly wrap your fingers around the handle and bend your wrist back toward your body.

Cradling can also protect the ball during a body check. When you see a defender approaching, turn so that you protect your stick with your body. The cradle motion here is a little different. Hold your stick fully upright and add more elbow motion to your cradle. As you cradle, watch the defender—not the ball—and look for an **open** *teammate.*

Catching

Catching is more difficult in lacrosse than in many other sports because you can grab and hold the ball with only your stick's netting. The ball moves fast, so you must always keep your eyes on it. You must also know how to handle your stick to keep the ball from bouncing out of the netting.

Making the catch

A big part of catching is being ready for the pass. Hold your stick upright and in front of the shoulder of your top hand, with the netting facing the passer. Your top hand should be near the middle of the shaft. Keep your eyes on the pass until the ball reaches your stick's netting, and move your stick back quickly to cushion the ball's impact. This movement keeps the ball from bouncing out of the pocket.

Remember to keep your eyes on the ball instead of on your stick.

Keep practicing

Have a friend toss the ball toward you to test your catching skill. As your catching improves, try catching the ball as you jog toward the pass. During a game, you'll have to be able to catch on the run.

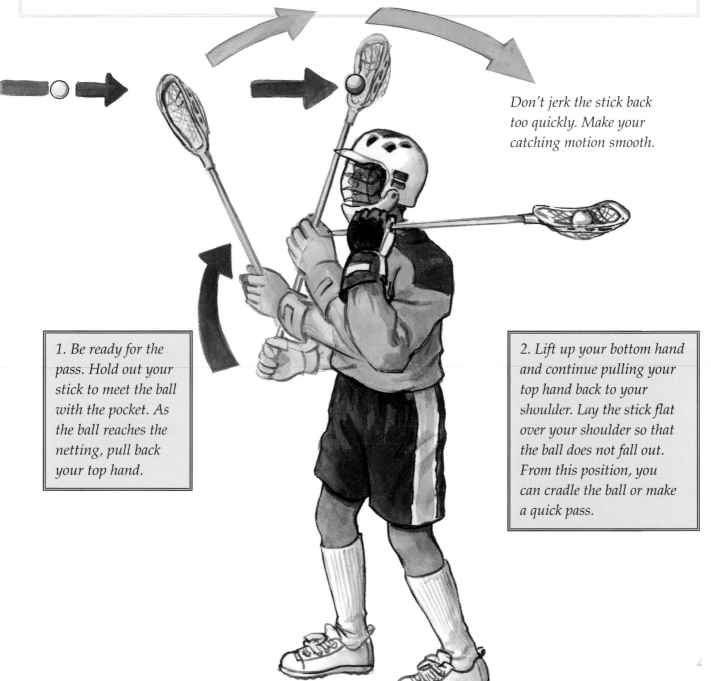

Don't jerk the stick back too quickly. Make your catching motion smooth.

1. Be ready for the pass. Hold out your stick to meet the ball with the pocket. As the ball reaches the netting, pull back your top hand.

2. Lift up your bottom hand and continue pulling your top hand back to your shoulder. Lay the stick flat over your shoulder so that the ball does not fall out. From this position, you can cradle the ball or make a quick pass.

Passing

Once you catch the ball, it won't be long before you need to get rid of it again! Your opponents will check you quickly. The best way to help your team is to pass the ball often. Passing keeps your team in control of the ball and the game. It is important that you learn to aim your passes, or your opponents may **intercept**, or catch the ball instead. When aiming your pass, stand sideways with the shoulder of your bottom hand toward your target. Always watch your target! Keep your hands close together but not touching. This closeness gives you more control over the direction of your pass. Cradle the ball so that it's in the pocket of your stick instead of the throat.

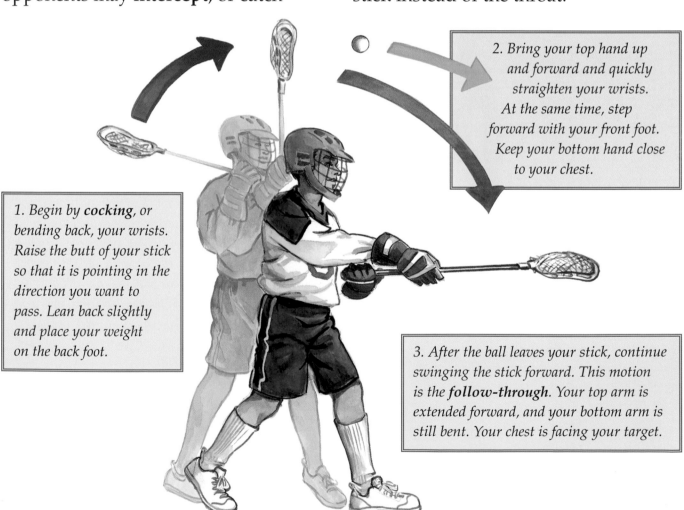

1. Begin by **cocking**, or bending back, your wrists. Raise the butt of your stick so that it is pointing in the direction you want to pass. Lean back slightly and place your weight on the back foot.

2. Bring your top hand up and forward and quickly straighten your wrists. At the same time, step forward with your front foot. Keep your bottom hand close to your chest.

3. After the ball leaves your stick, continue swinging the stick forward. This motion is the **follow-through**. Your top arm is extended forward, and your bottom arm is still bent. Your chest is facing your target.

Passing fancy

The best way to improve your passing is to practice with a partner. Begin by standing about fifteen feet (4.5 m) apart and passing the ball back and forth. Focus on making good, solid catches and smooth passes—don't rush anything! As you become more comfortable, try passing on the run. Don't sprint—jog briskly up the field, staying about fifteen feet (4.5 m) apart. This drill helps you learn how to pass to a moving target, which you will do often in a game.

When passing on the run, aim your pass a little ahead of your teammate so that he or she can meet it without slowing down. If the pass arrives a little behind, the player has to turn back, and an opponent could reach the ball first.

Taking aim

Well-aimed passes can be difficult to make at first. If you find your passes are too high or too low for your partner to catch, try some of these troubleshooting tips:

- Be sure the ball is in the shooting pocket of the netting. A ball passed from the throat will be released late and low.

- Try changing the speed of your swing and see what happens. Experiment by moving your top hand slightly up or down the handle.

- Make certain that only your top arm is extending forward during your swing. Your bottom arm stays bent through the whole motion.

Chasing the ball

Lacrosse is a fast-paced game with many **loose balls**. A ball is loose when neither team has control of it. Sometimes a rough check knocks the ball out of a player's stick. At other times, a missed pass ends with the ball falling to the ground. Whatever the reason, chasing down and grabbing a loose ball is an important skill to learn.

Here's the scoop

In order to grab a ball off the ground, you must **scoop** it up. Get close to the ball by bending low. Being close helps you judge your scoop. If the ball is bouncing or rolling, try to get in front of its path. Whatever the ball's direction, chase it down—don't let the ball get away!

1. Step close to the ball and bend at the knees and hips. Look only at the ball. Put your top hand near the stick's throat and reach down. Push forward with your bottom hand and scoop the tip of the stick under the ball.

2. When the ball is in the pocket, straighten your hips and knees. Cradle the ball to keep it safe while you look at what's happening around you. Check for any open teammates or a clear path on the field. You can then pass the ball or run to a better position.

Using your body

Scooping up loose balls during a game isn't easy! The ball often bounces unpredictably, and you will have to race your opponent to scoop it first. To get the best position for scooping, use your body as a blocker. As you approach the ball, step quickly between it and your opponent. Use your bottom to push your opponent farther out of the way. Continue protecting the ball with your body as you scoop it up.

Get someone to toss and roll balls to you and practice scooping them up. Don't try to scoop up the ball with only one hand on your stick. You need both hands for control.

Arriving late

As hard as you try, you won't always be the first player to reach a loose ball. Even if your opponent gets to it first, you can check his or her stick and **dislodge**, or knock out, the ball. Get your stick under your opponent's stick as he or she lifts up the ball. Raise your stick upward to tap the opponent's stick, and the ball may come loose. Fight hard for the ball, but never check your opponent from behind. You can get a major penalty, which hurts you and your team—and your opponent will get the ball!

When trying to the win the ball, be aggressive and confident, but play by the rules. You must be within five feet (1.5 m) of the ball before you can check your opponent.

Face-offs and draws

Every lacrosse game involves quick showdowns at the center of the field. In box lacrosse and boys' field lacrosse, the showdown is called a face-off. In girls' field lacrosse, it is called a draw. Although these plays are different, they occur at the same times: at the start of the game, at the start of a new quarter or half, and after goals are scored. Centers are the only players who perform face-offs or draws. Once the ball is placed between the two centers, the official blows a whistle to start the play, and the centers compete for control of the ball.

"Okay pardner, draw!"

In field lacrosse, girls perform draws standing up. The centers stand facing one another with their right shoulders pointing toward their own goaltenders. The umpire sets up their sticks so that the netting overlaps. He or she then places the ball between the netting of the two sticks. As the whistle blows, the players quickly lift their sticks, and the ball flies upward. Both centers fight to catch the ball as it comes down.

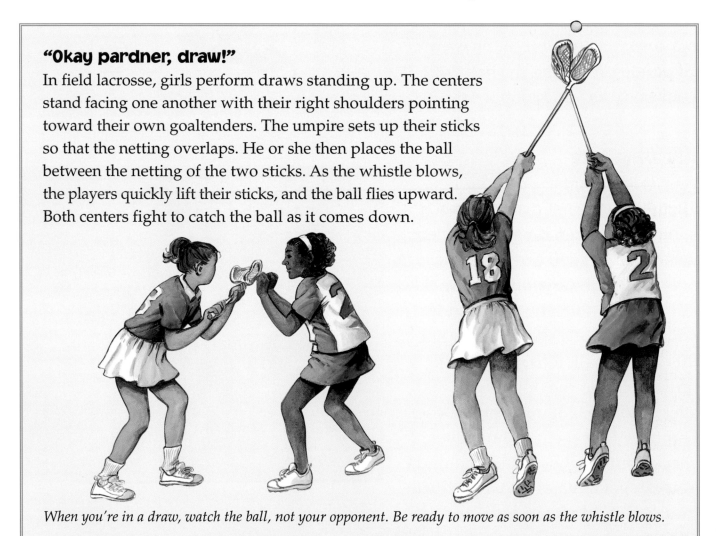

When you're in a draw, watch the ball, not your opponent. Be ready to move as soon as the whistle blows.

Get down!

Face-offs are done from a squatting position. In this position, each center's left shoulder faces the opposing team's goalie. Some centers like to squat low with their knees fully bent. Others prefer to bend mostly at the waist. The players hold their sticks side by side and flat on the ground. The ball is placed between the sticks, and the players turn their pockets to face away from it. Try different face-off positions until you find which works best for you.

*Lean forward over your stick and watch the ball. As soon as the whistle blows, **clamp**, or trap, the ball with the back of your stick. Quickly drag it back toward you. The faster you move, the better your chances of getting the ball will be!*

Waiting for the ball

Draws and face-offs are the sole duty of the centers. In fact, sometimes other players cannot move until the showdown is over. In boys' field lacrosse, all players except the wingers must be still until one of the centers wins possession of the ball. In box lacrosse, the other players can move, but they are not allowed to enter the large center circle until the ball moves out of the smaller face-off circle. In girls' field lacrosse, the other players must wait until the ball leaves the center circle before they can touch it.

They score!

Since the team with the most points wins, scoring is the ultimate objective in lacrosse. To score, you must shoot the ball at the net. Shooting is not the same as passing—you don't want the other person to catch the ball! Good shots are hard, fast, and aimed at open spots on the net. Remember, if you shoot from inside the goalie's crease, the goal won't count.

Fooled you!

Before you can shoot, you have to get past your opponents and close to the net. A **fake**, shown below left, is a basic way to fool a nearby defender. Another tricky move is the **pivot**, shown below right. There are other moves that will get you past opponents, but these two are good starting points.

Fake

1. Your feet are the most important part of the fake. Once you're near the defender, step quickly to the left with your left foot. Lean to the left with your upper body.

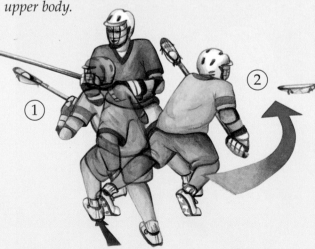

2. When the defender moves to cover you, take a large step right. Use a burst of speed to run around the defender. Your opponent is moving backward, so it is difficult for him or her to follow you.

Pivot

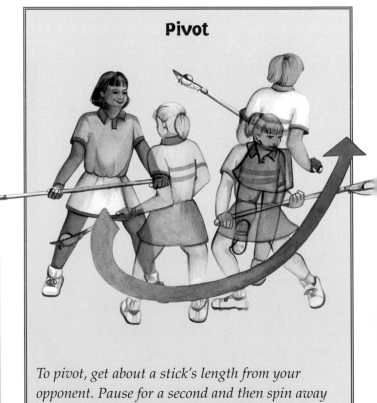

To pivot, get about a stick's length from your opponent. Pause for a second and then spin away quickly to the right or left around the defender. Sprint away to a good shooting position.

Take a shot

Always shoot with the ball in the pocket and near the tip of your stick. Doing so gives you the best aim. Try one of these basic shots to get you started.

Sidearm shots can make it easier to shoot around a defender. For a sidearm shot, put both hands near the butt of your stick. To shoot, swing your stick around your top hand's side at waist level. For extra power, twist at the waist as you shoot.

The overhand shot is similar to the passing motion shown on page 20, but the movement is faster and harder. Remember to start with your weight on your back foot. Step farther forward during the shot than you do for a pass. Cock your wrists for extra power and follow through fully.

Target practice

You can improve your aim by practicing on your own. If you don't have a net, draw one on an outdoor wall with chalk. Add targets in the spots shown on the right and practice hitting them. Try shooting from different distances and angles. Work to perfect your shooting motion so you can do it quickly. The faster your shots are, the less time a goalie will have to react.

Strong defense

A good defender is patient, watchful, and ready to react to an opponent's mistake. Defensive skills aren't just useful for defenders, however. All players should learn how to check an opponent properly. Practicing simple defensive skills such as running backward and sidestepping will help you become a better player.

Stick up and ready

Good defense starts with a strong **ready stance**. Hold your stick out in front of you with both hands. Have your top hand near the middle of the handle. Turn the stick's pocket toward your opponent. Crouch lower than your opponent and have your knees flexed so that you're ready to spring in any direction. It's easier to keep your balance when your body is low.

Patience

As a defender, your main objective is to stay between your opponent and the net. Don't rush to meet your opponent. If you move forward too quickly, the player can fake and then run around you. You can also avoid fakes by watching the center, not the feet, of your opponent's body. Be patient and wait for the right time to make a move.

Stick it to 'em

You make a **stick check**, shown top right, when you hit your opponent's stick to try to knock the ball loose. It is the main check female field players use. In girls' field lacrosse, the check must be done in front of the opponent. In boys' field lacrosse, players can stick check from anywhere as long as they do not slash anyone.

After you knock the ball loose, chase it and scoop it up.

Wait for the right moment

Stick checks are useful but also risky. If you miss the check, it's easy for your opponent to run around you as you lunge forward. Try to stick check when your opponent is a little distracted, such as when he or she is looking around to make a pass.

When opponents get by you, don't give up! Chase them and wait for them to shoot or pass. Remember, stick checking from behind may not be allowed in your league!

Giving a body check

Body checks are more forceful than stick checks. They are useful when a player is running alongside the ball carrier. To make a body check, bump your shoulder against your opponent and knock him or her off balance. The check must hit the opponent from the front or the side. The body contact must be above the waist and below the shoulders. Players get penalties for illegal checks.

The box goalie's stance is slightly crouched with bent knees. The stick is held near the throat with the top hand only. The stick's netting is between the legs. The shoulders help block the net's corners.

Field lacrosse nets are taller than box lacrosse nets, so the goalies must stand up straighter. They hold their sticks in both hands with the netting in front of one shoulder. In this position, the stick is ready to catch high shots.

Goaltending

Unlike other players, goaltenders don't move around the field. The position requires concentration and quick reflexes, as well as slightly different skills than those needed by other players. Field goalies have larger nets to protect than goalies in box lacrosse have. Box goalies wear more pads.

The perfect stance

Like any defensive player, goalies have a basic ready stance. The stance protects the net and keeps the goalie ready to spring into action. Box and field lacrosse goalies use different stances, as shown on the left.

Keeping track of the ball

It is important to follow the movement of the ball as your opponents close in on the net. Don't make any moves that will put you off balance. Always watch a shooter's stick and upper body. Follow the shooter with your body, but make your motions smooth and relaxed. Be ready to move in any direction as you back toward the net. Don't make a big move until you are sure the shot is being taken.

Sometimes a goalie moves too far away from the net when challenging shooters. The shooter can then pass to a teammate, who can easily shoot into the open net. Come out, but not too far.

Covering the angles

When you're in net, you need to challenge a shooter by **covering the angles**. Come a few steps out of the net in your ready stance, with your shoulders facing the shooter. By coming out, you reduce the number of places from which the shooter can make a good shot, so you can block more of the net.

Good goalie tips

Don't be afraid to use your body to stop a shot. A goalie should make every effort to make a save!

C When catching lower shots, get your leg behind the stick for extra blocking protection.

C Stay aware of all opponents near the net, even if they don't have the ball. If one of them receives a pass, you must move quickly to cover them.

C As soon as you catch a shot, look for an open teammate up the field. If you can make a good pass, you can get your team quickly into a scoring position. Just be careful there are no opponents nearby to intercept the pass!

Your stick is the best tool for stopping shots. Always try to catch a shot instead of just blocking it.

31

Glossary

Note: Boldfaced words defined in the book may not appear in the glossary.

arena A building with an enclosed area for playing a sport

attack half The half of the playing field that contains the opposing team's net

check To knock or bump a player's stick or body to get control of the ball

draw A start of play during which two players face each other and try to get the ball first

face-off A start of play during which two players crouch down facing each other and try to get the ball first

follow-through To continue to swing your lacrosse stick forward after the ball is released

goal The point given for sending the ball into the net

loose ball Describing a lacrosse ball when neither team is in control of it

major foul The breaking of an important rule

mark To guard certain players and prevent them from passing the ball or scoring

minor foul The breaking of a less important rule, which results in a lesser punishment than a major foul

net A rectangular metal frame with string mesh, in which goals are scored

open To be available to receive a pass

penalty box The area where players who have broken rules must sit for a certain period of time

position The responsibilities and playing area assigned to a particular player

power play When one team has the advantage of having more players on the field

ready stance The body position used when preparing for action

short-handed Describing a team that has a penalty and is playing with fewer than the normal number of players

Index

3 4 5 6 7 8 9 0 Printed in the U.S.A. 2 1 0 9 8 7 6 5